UEA MA Creative Writing Anthologies 2015: Poetry

UEA POETRY 2015

First published by Egg Box Publishing 2015

International © 2015 retained by individual authors.

This book is sold subject to the condition that it shall not, by way of trade or otherwise, be lent, resold, hired out, stored in a retrieval system, or otherwise circulated without the publisher's prior consent in any form of binding or cover other than that in which it is published and without a similar condition including this condition being imposed on the subsequent purchaser.

A CIP record for this book is available from the British Library.

UEA POETRY 2015 is typeset in Adobe Garamond. Titles are set in Mercury.

Cover photography from the photographic unit, UEA.

Printed and bound in the UK by Imprint Digital.

Designed and typeset by Sean Purdy.

Proofread by Sarah Gooderson.

Distributed by Central Books.

ISBN: 978-0-9932962-2-2

Acknowledgements

Thanks are due to the School of Literature, Drama and Creative Writing at UEA in partnership with Egg Box Publishing for making the UEA MA Creative Writing anthologies possible.

We'd also like to thank the following people:

Tiffany Atkinson, John Boyne, Andrew Cowan,
Helen Cross, Giles Foden, Sarah Gooderson,
Rachel Hore, Kathryn Hughes, Catrina Laskey,
Bill Manhire, Jean McNeil, Natalie Mitchell,
Jeremy Noel-Tod, Beatrice Poubeau, Rob Ritchie,
Sophie Robinson, Helen Smith, Henry Sutton,
Val Taylor, Ian Thomson, Steve Waters,
Frances Wilson and Peter Womack.

Nathan Hamilton at Egg Box Publishing, and Sean Purdy.

Editorial team:

Rob Atkinson
Sohini Basak
Gill Blanchard
Jemma Carter
Joanna Graham
Alexis Kuzma
Elizabeth Lewis-Williams
Emma Victoria Miller
Molly Morris
Kayla Schmidt
Jade Tremblay
Chloe L Yeoh

CONTENTS

Introduction —————————————— 07
Tiffany Atkinson

Contributors:

Charlie Annis ———————————————— 13

Sohini Basak ————————————————— 19

Christopher Clark ————————————— 27

Billy Head ————————————————————— 35

Zoe Kingsley ———————————————— 43

Bee Sparks ————————————————— 49

Chloe L Yeoh ———————————————— 57

TIFFANY ATKINSON

Introduction

IT IS A PLEASURE TO INTRODUCE THE WORK OF THIS YEAR'S MA POETRY cohort, and I hope that you will enjoy reading this poetry as much as I have enjoyed watching it grow and crystallise. Sceptics of the creative writing workshop are apt to suggest that the teaching environment breeds homogeneity and dull consensus, but as if the poetry doesn't speak clearly enough for itself, let me assure you that this year's workshops were anything but a dull consensus. Tutors always learn a great deal from a committed and lively group, and these poems might be read collectively as a record of some stimulating and provocative conversations about what poetry can do. Each of these poets has worked hard and generously to forge not only his or her own distinctive style but to support and encourage the discoveries of their peers, and being part of this process is surely one of the richest rewards of teaching creative writing. This is my first year of teaching at UEA so I feel a particular bond with these writers. They have been a wonderful introduction to the university, and in years to come I hope it will be my privilege to look back and say, *I knew them when...*

Poetry can be a subversive activity, not least in the way it rethinks and puts askance familiar cultural narratives or orthodoxies. Charlie Annis's poems take on the cadences of scripture to give us 'Satan the dazzler, the Copper King / the high-wire hoofman / Satan the unmistakable, sloughed in sour juices / like a black spot on the sun.' This is playful writing, yes; but never facile: these poems are both knowing and interrogative, a suite of contemporary apocrypha.

All poems are little linguistic environments that take the reader into unfamiliar and often surprising territory. Sohini Basak's poetry especially creates an engrossing unmapped world between memory and story, fact and imagination, married with a gentle wit and an acute eye for detail. Don't be fooled by the mellifluous syntax: these poems are full of little barbs – 'to think that / these trees have not moved even an inch all this while' – that will catch unawares and resonate long after reading.

Christopher Clark's poems are intensely alert to the dissonances of contemporary textual culture, and make deft use of found material to dramatise these encounters on the page. His work is also alive to the fickleness of the brain's functioning, often leading him into gently surreal imagery that delivers the poem's power of everyday strangeness: 'In offices with plastic trees, we oscillate / from aslant eyes, trickle over / their green tongues and try to lick the residual tides / of water window streams.'

The markings of a poem on the page are always a dynamic between utterance and silence, the ventured and the unspoken. Billy Head's poems are acutely aware of this, using the white space dynamically to suggest the force of individual and cultural repressions, or framing incidental detail to gesture towards a more troubled understory: 'At the Bank of Africa / ATM this morning / people queued / with their eyes shut / then groped for the lips / of the cubicle door…' Read these poems for their silences as well as their utterance: a reminder that absence may have a signifying weight of its own.

Zoe Kingsley's work responds wittily to the provocative and recently revived question of poetry's 'relevance'. Her response is an immersion poetics that places the writer speculatively at the centre of a network of uncertain but registered significances, from public art – 'I circle / the chalk dome and forum square / around inanimate wax figurines' to the banal vicissitudes of 'home loans, filing cabinets and / a broken-down fridge.' Her second poem by contrast is a triumph of economy and sensitivity to the lapidary quality of language stripped down to its working parts. Expansion and contraction: almost a lesson in the scope of technique.

Bee Sparks's poems have such a flair for the cadences of spoken language that they almost read as monologues, but contain such twists and edges that you will want to read them again to catch the full weight of their strangeness: 'last i saw she was / trying to do lines off the cloth curve / of a deck chair   but / i came home on sunday and haven't been back since.' Sharp and deadpan, these poems are also attuned to the understated power of the sudden gear-shift: 'behind her the reeds / tangle upwards towards the / arch of the sky / *the kind of mess that would never / make it to England.*' The apparent smoothness of form again veils an unsettling tonal complexity.

Poets have always drawn on shared cultural resources like artworks and fable to explore their own imaginative reach. Chloe L Yeoh does both of these. In an ekphrastic poem after Dali's 'Homage to Newton' she finds fresh ways of metabolising images of the heart/apple/globe with an intensity that illustrates the wonderful capacity of metaphor to have it all at once in a brief instant of multiple vision. Elsewhere she mines the disturbing subtexts of legend and folk-tale, again using startling figurative language as if to prove the enduring power of the 'new bottle' to give renewed contemporary resonance: 'Mother's love was geological: / like swallowing diamonds, / like shaving chalk.'

In conclusion, I wish each of these contributors the very best as they continue their writing lives beyond their time at UEA. I hope that they keep in touch with us and, more importantly, with each other: all writers need a supportive critical community and I like to think that one has begun here (but who will bring the biscuits?).

UEA MA Creative Writing Anthologies 2015: Poetry

CHARLIE ANNIS

Satan considers the fruits

In excelsis

Satan awakes from his fall

Satan's answer to Job

From the Sayings of
the Desert Fathers

Satan considers the fruits

Satan bit the head off a banana
mashed it round his mouth a couple of times
and spat it out.

> *Too modest*
> he said

Satan skinned an orange
and stood it on the table, naked.

> *Too naive*
> he said

Satan strapped a pear onto a broomstick
and slipped it under a woman's skirt.

> *Too stoical*
> he said

Satan clamped a grapefruit in a vice
and necked the run-off with a flourish.

> *Too progressive*
> he said

Satan went bare-knuckled with a pomegranate
till it split and spat its teeth out.

> *Too spiritual*
> he said

Satan put a mango in a wig
and called it 'Mother'.

> *Too unhappy*
> he said

In excelsis

Satan came to the mouth of the cave and set his lamp down.

The day's devotions were already underway:
a string of voices sounding high up in the cirriform
fusing ozone out of simple air
                with their bright hosannas
the angelic ecstasy of altitude.

Yes, that was how He liked it: aqueous, inert
the Zen harmonics in the firmament
the stately music of the spheres.

It was said of Fr Vincenzo Lombardi
such was the purity of his nature
that at certain moments in the Church's year
(Jupiter in its second orbit round the sun)
at prayer the sharper-eared among his brethren could detect
a low continuous hum
reverberating from his reverend head
like a finger on the wet rim of a wine glass.

Satan awakes from his fall

Shit-mouthed, trouserless
spreadeagled on the bare floor
his creased skin tingling and turning numb
on the unforgiving carpet

Satan the dazzler, the Copper King
the high-wire hoofman
Satan the unmistakable, sloughed in sour juices
like a black spot on the sun

'I want to feel like Hiroshima' he had said
and sipped his drink, a flat pitch for the waitress
the rough journey of his hands
through sweat and clasp and silk, the tears.

Satan's answer to Job

And the LORD answered Job out of the whirlwind
the ground rippled, birds exploded.

Satan sighed and flicked away his cigarette,
took out a small pink card and read aloud:

You have won Second Prize in a beauty contest
Collect £10. Do not pass GO.

From the Sayings of the Desert Fathers

Two brothers came from Scetis to Abba Satan and said to him 'Abba, give us a word.' But the old man said nothing and the brothers went away distressed. The next day the brothers came again and said to him 'Abba, give us a word' but still the old man said nothing. The brothers came a third time and said 'Abba, give us a word.' At this, the old man cocked his leg and farted loudly in their faces. And the two brothers went away greatly encouraged.

Charlie Annis is training to become an Anglican priest in West Yorkshire.

SOHINI BASAK

Lesser Himalayas

a helium balloon overtakes us
as we ride the Ferris wheel

the stains on the tablecloth
are trying to say something

Engrammatic

Setting

Islander

Lesser Himalayas

Safe in the greenhouse
you warm up
to the sycophant orchids

while I see nothing
but fir lined yaks suffering
in bulky silence.

You measure one bird
at a time but if you stretched out
beyond the softness of rhododendrons

I could show you
sweaters shrink or nudge a fire
and threadbare dragons who will not

surrender. You have framed
them all and these hills are impossible
islands under your facile shoes

rail tracks disappear behind
sharper pines closing anthers –
the hills are frowning, it is night.

a helium balloon overtakes us as we ride the Ferris wheel

From up there it was easy to point at things
so easy to decide where to go next: we would do
everything that we weren't allowed. We would
get not two but four tickets to the freak show tent
and go in twice, in succession, just to make sure
that the four-headed calf was no contraption, we
would eat the twisted jilipi, its syrup, fuchsia
spinning in our cotton candies, and beguni with its oil.
We would watch the daredevil motorcyclists up close
as they orbited the inside of a giant disco ball, and cheer,
after all we had come together at the old February fair-
ground after years of being away and who knows when
the pandal would be made out of peanut shells again; so we
made a map in motion which shifted with our counter-clock
seats, and I felt my stomach grow giddy with gravity or plain
joy. When we got off after three rounds, the ground still
revolved and I said how odd it was that everything looked
smaller, the fairground must have shrunk in these ten years
and when we lined up in the last tent with exact change
for four tickets, my brother suddenly said – to think that
these trees have not moved even an inch all this while.

the stains on the tablecloth are trying to say something

Again I have taken to listening to conversations
I don't understand, languages I will never learn
I tell myself that this eavesdropping
is for research only, perhaps it will
generate some poetry, language begets
language and – immediately the world
swells up, and I begin to see how syllables
can bounce out of toasters, or are dropped delicately
to dissolve in tea cups, how vowels fall through
the fine holes of a colander, phrases you want
to swallow whole made of sounds that shine,
a globule of light at the end of spoons, those
bits of table talk I try very hard to catch between
my fingers or chopsticks, delicious amateur nothings.

Engrammatic

time has been strange to me today three year old days returning in backyards with plastic chairs dogs sniffing paper plates and everybody singing. the wind is blowing but the wind is always blowing you are here or there you are or elbows touching or the tree opposite the photocopy shop is baring stiff branches but this is the great repeating act the annual suspense before it bursts into flowers white with delicate yellowing and you are frowning and i am losing your attention thinking white flowers smell hackneyed with remembrance but go stand beneath the tree when they come back and you will see through cycles. someone else somewhere is playing a memory and don't you think it would be sad if we look away shut the windows and boil down everything to coincidence. i have been strange to time today. the wind is blowing and it is always blowing dust into this room and the dust gathers gathers gathers for me to etch names or these dates.

Setting

These are those landscapes of books read during summer holidays these are those landscapes in stories about other summer holidays but here are the landscapes within my reach I am walking through them although I cannot call each tree by its name but sometimes one slips out of my mouth a flash in brown and blue like the jay who visits my afternoon window who will perch on the same birch sycamore oak dogwood suspecting a fox among berries and brambles who turns out to be a highway deer – they are all here now but long ago I would spend afternoons wondering how soft foxgloves would be to touch in the sharp of a certain country wind for the pages of the borrowed school library books were more or less the same degree of papery which translated during the first months as nearness filmed over as elsewhere and what I saw of England I saw in ink sketches in pencil lined pages on the opposite sides of stories.

Islander

What the thunder did not say:
>   no one wants to turn
>   into a river overnight.

The streets lay still, dry,
>   still undercover of last season's
>   pinecones that wanted to be picked up.

Woodsmoke led me out. I come bearing
>   kindling enough to build
>   a fire to burn all my boats.

Sohini Basak is from India and has been published in *Litro, Ambit, The Ofi Press, Paris Lit Up, Helter Skelter*. She won second prize at the inaugural *RædLeaf India Poetry Prize* and was shortlisted for the *Melita Hume Poetry Prize* in 2014. She is currently working on her first poetry collection.

CHRISTOPHER CLARK

How-to-Poem

Dead Ideas (And Grand Applications)

A Mother's Struggle in Lecture Notes

Romance Titles

Therapy

North Circular

How-to-Poem

Find the starting point.
        Scan the page, stalk line widths,
chart the movement from A
        to B. Insert a metaphor, manage
line breaks. Create associations and/or
        dissonance whereby the sense of the poem
can be subverted. Explore expansion of fields
        and experiment with contraction of
range. Imagine a lake, or interior starting point
        moving between the borders of the two.
Make them porous, or rigid and tie armless hands
        behind your back. Mourn the lost
set aside whilst a dog whines over pancakes in the
        corner. Think of all the voices
that speak out like badly formed a cappella. The tenor
        is an octave higher than he should be.
In offices with plastic trees, we oscillate
        from aslant eyes, trickle over
their green tongues and try to lick the residual tides
        of window water streams.

Dead Ideas (And Grand Applications)

This is your final resting place, post-slip
through synapses of my fingertips. I wish
I'd been able to sketch the easy dimension
of us as we hurtled through cityscapes: its aged
tin-cans promised sixty, but grated along at more
like twenty. They are like grasping at gummy atoms,
strands pulling fabric. So I'll try and cut shapes from
something more concrete. Something pretty and great,
like the Eiffel or Leaning Tower of Pisa. Something
profound like the Sistine Chapel. I just wish
to cannibalise Michelangelo. But all I can think
of is caught and nothing's moving: physicists tell us
static charges are always hardest to push from stand-still.
It's probably why so many of us jump from buildings,
or stick our heads inside Easy Homebake ovens.

A Mother's Struggle in Lecture Notes

Tom's goodness and Mr Shelby, benevolent master, overcome to tears [these are female connections]. Helpful farmer Eliza: 'Lord bless you.'
Is the realist style too invasive? 'We must take leave.'
Eliza is desolate, forlorn by maternal love.
Is the ability for her to pass important to the story?
[Direct address to the reader]: 'If I were you…'
Tom leaves the home – as plantation? Why invoke the passage of Atlantic trade in microcosm from New Orleans to rural Louisiana?
Trauma of the river journey, red. Miss Ophelia is treadin' on 'em, one asleep behind the door, like litter. Lack of origins (mother, place of birth etc.) and religious education – why?
We don't know anything about time. Slavery skewers temporality.

Romance Titles

Finally, I shall compare thee
Extremely loud and incredibly close
Speaking toward you
Touching, feeling
Across the black Atlantic
An adventure in form
You, the queer child
And me, alien
Versus predator
This emperor waltz we do
Attempt to break it down
Over the hours of bloodroot
The tracks of your cherry ghost
Play it as less than zero.

Therapy

I did what you said: tried to lie out my submission
Over sheets used now for sleeping dust
After many sixty-dollar sessions, you said to salvage
To try and gather some of our swept-up fraction
Discover the reasons for our dislocation
Kept packaged amongst fields of 'unconscious machinery'

To rediscover unity one must act like machinery
To resolve oneself to utter submission
To imagine what it's like to be a fleck of dust
To lie amongst the body and its salvage
To deliberate over working through our fractions
To let us have each other's ego to dislocate

You said I was a bone you wanted to dislocate
Inside all I felt like was machinery
Only ever interested in yet another submission
That lay along by the others gathering dust
A market of words sold for more useless salvage
Worth as much as a bottom-priced fraction

You both lost the 'r' somewhere in your fraction
Your two ideas of each another began to dislocate
And now you're both working like machinery
Meant for some different purpose or submission
Your gears have become stuck, choked by dust
And you listen less, feeling there's nothing to salvage

I ask what's the need for this salvage?
We work better as separate fractions
From one another, no point to role-reverse and dislocate
Accept it, we're just damaged machinery
From one another, give in to this final submission
As it cries out to us, sick from pumping its dust

It worries us when we can't see for the weight of dust
We lose sight of what it is we're trying to salvage
here, and forget what it was like before any kind of fraction
before we become lost amongst all of our dislocating
built up from the mechanism of our defensive machinery
to protect one another, we need to become the other's submission.

North Circular

Three. My cerebral cortex misplaced his thesaurus. So I asked him
to look around for it last Motuwehurisunday, or maybe I didn't
ask him at all – let me think – when his synapses fire, he looks like
a digestive tract with IBS. 'It's hard to find something
without any limbs,' he complained. I feel him rattle my head, toy-plastic
spray in the – what is it? – embalming fluid – that's not it, just give me
an extra millisecond…
nope – anyway, he looked in his, uh my, memory
bank but the teller said they'd already SEALED for the day. But,
what about the ATM? He makes some heavy RASPS [for effect I think]
makes his MEMBERS tip-tap the COUNTER one-two-three-four, one-two-
    three-four. What's
this? The collected work of SEAMUS FREUD.
—W
ait, who? [Some things aren't right here]
  —'
Never mind, there's no time! What's this?' One-two-three-four,
two-one-three a goldfish forgets every seven seconds [Wikipedia 1998] is a song
by Nenah Cherry [Sepia-tinged video] her brother was a bit of a one-hit-wonder
though 'what's this?' isn't getting us anywhere. Two-one-three-four, one-four-two-

---

Christopher Clark is a poet and performer, currently based in Norwich. He has previously been published in *Ink, Sweat & Tears*, *The Cadaverine* and *Ecstatic Peace Poetry Journal*. He has worked on commissions including for The Royal Philharmonic Society. He enjoys 90s TV, cheese and occasionally tweets @chriswillclark.

BILLY HEAD

Ilmenite Sands

Holes

Décollage

Lamba

Lamba ii

It

Ilmenite Sands

It's not been rough
like this —

the fishermen
aren't catching.

At the Bank of Africa
ATM this morning

people queued
with their eyes shut

then groped for the lips
of the cubicle door

and some quiet
to be slammed back

on the ocean
and all it brings.

Holes

in assorted
shapes and sizes
appeared in places
so intimately public
one day in February
but just a few

splinteringjacarandabark

                                                                                          up a
                                                                                          pillar

cut glass
                in
                    raindarkened
                        concrete

      pixelate
      crimson

                                                          in a
                                                          hotel

                                                                  in a home

Décollage

i.m. a pirate

Knows his 360 from the hip but kick him and he'll jump higher than you think blond dread and a beaten book with the appearance of being in his bag a long time before he discovered he was peacock in love spread his feathers one day and flew burnt cut bit by bit but thereafter belonging to the heat c'est une drogue shrugging his shoulders crouch the need to take a step back some don't even know they've been clac clac about a good wind that we're all pirates in this world matching nicotine breath always fingernails eaten short fidgety fingers off shortly to a terrain de bandits later found playing boo games with the street kids or on All Saints Day you see I'm on a very interesting axis des yeux super zoom tu vas pas à l'église toi? Oh yes I'll be saying bonjour Monsieur le Curé je vais tout confesser.

Lamba

                                                    not

                                              dyed and

                                        degummed but

                                       still coarse wiry

                                       and of its own

                                        colour landy

                                      gasy disintegrates

                                      at about the same

                                       speed as human

                                    flesh so that a body

                                       once bound in it

                                         and over time

                                      rebound becomes

                                     a mass of brown

                                        fibre becomes

                                    indistinguishable

                                          from silk

Lamba ii

mediated by
        cocoonsoak

                a hundred
              in a house of
              snores

              and

  pigfat fug
    in moistcrutch

              rough skin

    assured sleep

          sweet weak taf
          and
                mampalahelo
fa tsy maintsy mampalahelo
                  aloe

   furrowed shade
              aloka
  tapia green
      stickbamboo
      production lines

teased and spun and re-spun

              act of love and
sequins

       shrieking in the dank but
   which one is he
      hilltop crowding
    lopping

greasy meat and grease and

rest

It

For Mialy

You can't have seen it but your mum's face when you gave her a squeeze by the check-in desks was a face I'd seen once before, that morning we found the dog dead in the pool. It brought back a conversation I'd forgotten I had in 2007 not far away in Ambohidratrimo with a woman whose sister was living in Lyon. I must have asked this woman if she wanted to go there too. Her reply was silence then "yes but I hope I don't like it." I do wonder what went through your mum's head when she saw you looking for her in the car park ten minutes later because Air Mauritius didn't like the look of the long umbrella she'd repaired for you and insisted you took because you'd need it where you were going.

Billy Head teaches creative writing at the University of Antananarivo, Madagascar. This selection is part of a longer project for which he has secured research funding. *Holes* is a response to the killing of protestors in central Antananarivo on 7th February 2009. *Lamba* and *Lamba ii* are part of a sequence exploring the place of silk (*landy*) in relations between the living and the dead in Madagascar. Not all Billy's poems are about death!

ZOE KINGSLEY

'I think poetry has really rather
connived at its own irrelevance'

my bit

Episode one: analysis of the Bananafish-maker

Episode two: the wedge and jam jar, again

'I think poetry has really rather connived at its own irrelevance'

Jeremy, like some phantasmagoric apparition
      – literally: the page a dream.

With soft red beard and hair he appears
in my
      opic vision as I circle
      the chalk dome and forum square
      around inanimate wax figurines.

    Like a vision
        pure and gold-wheatened
        a piece of Soviet propaganda.

        And it all arrives at a point:
        a link to *The Guardian*.

        While I argue for the importance of that one word
        anecdote: a cure for home loans, filing cabinets and
        a broken-down fridge.

my bit

a fuck

shaped

as a eu

phem

ism

a surface is a surface

it can swell   the warm

trunk in the bed pressed

up the side and laid

to rest the pillow slip forgetting

during the day   like Rothko

who probably knocked off

on the job at least once

or Goldberg scratching out S A R D I N E S

constantly walked in on   a pimply itch

just telling on its frame

Episode one: analysis of the Bananafish-maker

A started cigar-
ette on a window
sill.

The ash makes it
on the bottom of
the make-up bag

& no doubt on her
teeth upon reach-
ing Clapton to bru-

sh.

Episode two: the wedge and jam jar, again

The milk-eyed spot
underfoot by the
gutter. This leaking

vessel will
soon be mens-
truating on

the platform: hers
with a coffee rib-
bed mouth.

Zoe Kingsley is from Melbourne, Australia. She is associate editor for *The Suburban Review* and poetry co-editor for *Lighthouse*. Her poetry can be found at *The Suburban Review*, *The Bohemyth*, and inside the pages of various literary zines in both hemispheres.

BEE SPARKS

crummy.

workshop.

kinks.

pops.

pals.

apparition.

crummy.

i say we're only throwing her an intervention if there'll be banners and balloons   purple sparkly ones or you may as well not bother
the banner just says *wino* in all caps and would have been in comic sans if it were easier to replicate in giant foot high font   i construct a flattened pyramid of empty bottles in the garden for bowling because a party's not a party without activities +
we make all kinds of tiny replicas of foods   miniature chicken nuggets tiny jelly portions   small spheres of mash potato   +   i file down cocktail sticks to get rid of the sharp edges   the banner goes off without a fucking hitch   unfurls and splatters glitter across the floor hazes it through the air in front of her as we shout surprise   personally i thought the candles were a bit tacky   i've always been one for a touch of class   and you're probably wondering if she's off the booze   last i saw she was trying to do lines off the cloth curve of a deck chair   but i came home on sunday and haven't been back since

workshop.

*and everyone's writing fucking trauma
narratives in second person these days*
you tell me this over coffee and
*sometimes you just need to get things off
your back I say you I mean not whoever's
writing the wanky trauma narratives* I
say cos it is pretty shitty when
someone else is nicking your idea
and *not that yours are wanky yours are
completely and entirely justified by the
text* I say and after that speech I
definitely deserve my flat white and
maybe a pastry   a blaklava   or
whatever the fuck they're called but
you're staring me down over the rim
of your tiny coffee cup *what do you
have against second person trauma
narratives anyway* and this is when I
knock over the table and vault the
spreadeagled dog and am out the
door and I don't even spill my coffee
on the way *I don't know* I say *I could
write you a list* I say *I never know if it
actually means you or me or I* I say *there
usually isn't an actual Second Person and
you spend the whole novel stressing about
it and if there is one then it's never
satisfying* I say + I keep talking and
you don't swallow the coffee in your
 mouth or move the cup from your
lips and there's steam floating up
over your face and the only
movement I can see is the twitch of
your jaw and your eyes struggling
with the steam your lips are getting

redder-and-wetter-redder-and-wetter-
until I make the 117th comment of
my tirade which happens to be a
flippant remark about Kafka and you
swallow and continue conversation
where you left off and I have a
sneaking suspicion you might have
swallowed for Foster-Wallace too

kinks.

so far I've amassed:
an outsize brooch of an undersize beaded flamingo raising one eyebrow
an intricate ink and watercolour drawing of a topless guy with way too many bulges and a
speech bubble saying *werk it gurrrl!!*
a miniature ceramic replica of the Yellow Submarine (sadly no Blue Meanies were included)
a butter dish covered in tiny silver bees that you thought would *make a great candle holder*
a scrabble piece reading B1
a badge made from a crushed Yorkshire teabag
a tiny discoball missing one and a half mirrored panels
a 20s powder box with New York carved into its surface and ancient blush crowding its corners
a black and white postcard picturing a close-up of Ringo Starr's nose

you send me novelty items every couple of months
the weight of each little package extending into some farcical tragedy   in which I don't know how to tell you that
I don't really like you anymore

pops.

I'd say I am absolutely the cuddling type and hope you are too / Just got outta' jail (for B.S. as usual) feeling a bit low on life. Spent Christmas & New Years sleeping in dumpsters, currently a bit beyond sick of persecution from po-lice / I'm getting skinny like an Ethiope & really could do with a protein-shake regiment, or at least some good-wholesome-company about now / looking for a wrestle buddy to play rough with me – manhandle me, beat me down, leg scissors / bear hugs til I pass out / I always enjoy having diapered friends to hang around with / My mother thinks I'm retarded LOL / I need a father figure to hang out with and do stuff with me that I didn't have a chance to do when I was younger / i will give u a nice car to drive let u learn about the business / please send message if u want to help me accomplish and succeed and I promise u wouldn't regret it ... put "succeed Craigslist" in subject line please someone reply to this / My (shrivelly, carbonised) heart isn't too broke-ass, to fix my saviour a breakfast worthy of Rachel Ray! /
Please be serious because I am serious / I have little patience for haters

(this is a found poem)

pals.

you tell me your only requirement is getting stuffed oh and maybe a mechanical arm so the funeral's that little bit more interactive *you should make the stuffing out of dollar bills so corpse-you can make it rain* I'm going to get cremated to Spice Up Your Life not for the dancing but so everyone feels as awkward crying as I always do *post death retribution* you say you send me a postcard where you've pasted your head onto the body of that woman from New Orleans who got taxidermied and went to her own funeral *(did-she-smell-did-she-smell-did-she-smell? clammy-ointment-stink)* she has a speech bubble *mo' money mo' problems* but your fictional funeral can't have my catchphrase all that you're getting is me front row wearing your bra all thanks to nearly having a threesome with Skippy in Greece except he was wearing his dead pal's hat

apparition.

Runway Mary's perpetual bow waits to greet me   stark white against the fields' tea-and-smoked-earth smudge *not green at all*   fenced-off in case someone makes a mad dash to cop a feel   some hefty lad straight off a stag *not so pure now*   she flanks the perimeter of this precision of planes and lines and lights   behind her the reeds tangle upwards towards the arch of the sky   *the kind of mess that would never make it to England*

Bee Sparks was born in London and grew up in Ireland. She writes poems about her pals, Ireland and stuff she finds in the dark corners of the internet.

CHLOE L YEOH

Gravity

Daphne

Juniper

Gravity

After Salvador Dali's 'Homage to Newton'

The beating heart is no joke. I have seen,
swung in its place, the short leash
of a pendulum weighing heavily,
ball and chain. In the space
of human conscience rests the weight of the world,
a head expanded on thick shoulders and thinning
wrists. Atlas has nothing on this stranger's
open crown. There is no shrinking ribcage – only the imagining
of our imagining of a geocentric world stayed
by a hand on a fallen apple at one man's feet.

Daphne

I want
to traffic in

Apollo's touch.
I'm told: do not

watch only from
your window. Do not

trade heart
for hymn.

I tripped and got
bushed, now

I'm deep-rooted,
branching out.

Juniper

Under this overgrowth,
bowed bark and pines
thin as spindles

this shrubbery turned tree
turned bone, our mother's
temple —

this garden keeps birds
like watchers of beasts:

this is how I know
you're not asleep.

Were you sleeping,
you would be breath,
and in the juniper

I would not see spines.

If mother was a knife's edge,
then you, my brother, were a turtledove.

Crafted for audio transparency,
our home bared its secrets
to the living.

You were the only one
living, you with your face
ripe as berries

crushed underfoot.

I hid from each caw
you cried
that shrivelled to silence

that made the world less transparent
when the colour of skin could alter

to the touch.

Mother was landlocked,
stuffing her mouth with berries
'til her belly swelled.

You were her spectral inverse,
trapped in the underworld, rueing
the juniper on your tongue,
waiting for someone

to sing you out.

                        You used to fling earthward
                        from trees to prove
                        that falling was an acquired skill.

                        There were no nets,
                        my arms too short a reach,
                        my body too young

                        to be a temple
                        to house the memory
                        of a sighted body

                        folding itself in half.

You were so outbound,
where could I go but in?

Was it my silence,
my too-late grief?

A part of me followed
you under the tree.

Fault became me,
became your bones
that outweighed me,

that refused to stay buried,
that instead became birdsong,
taking the redeye out.

                              Mother's love was geological:
                              like swallowing diamonds,
                              like shaving chalk.

                              She was a sea of pearls
                              after a long dive, mercurial
                              and chipped as chiselled marble.

                              I was consolation at best,
                              my eyes slated like yours,
                              mundane as millstone,

                              a weighted sight.

Shrines do nothing
for the dead
but house them
in cocoons
of white and grey.

You left behind
so little, the urn
was lighter
than a dove's nest,
a thicket of pine.

There were
not enough
bones left
to form even
the outline of a bird.

                              All I have of you
                              is sculpted ash, a finger
                              of salt. In the stories
                              there were no singed clothes,
                              no scent of the rot
                              that rose from your body,
                              no sight of a brother
                              who turned from bird
                              to empty space.

Chloe L Yeoh lives in Malaysia. She was the inaugural recipient of the Bryan Heiser Memorial Bursary. Her work has appeared in *Lighthouse Literary Journal* and elsewhere.